GET YOUR ANIMALS IN ORDER

by Michael Bright

illustrated by Gavin Scott

WAYLAND

Natural History Museum

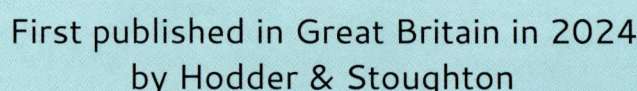

First published in Great Britain in 2024
by Hodder & Stoughton

Credits
Editor: Victoria Brooker
Designer: Peter Scoulding

HB ISBN: 978 1 5263 2233 3
PB ISBN: 978 1 5263 2234 0
EBK ISBN: 978 1 5263 2631 7

Printed in China

MIX
Paper | Supporting
responsible forestry
FSC® C104740

Wayland
An imprint of
Hachette Children's Group
Part of Hodder & Stoughton
Carmelite House
50 Victoria Embankment
London EC4Y 0DZ

An Hachette UK Company
www.hachette.co.uk
www.hachettechildrens.co.uk

CONTENTS

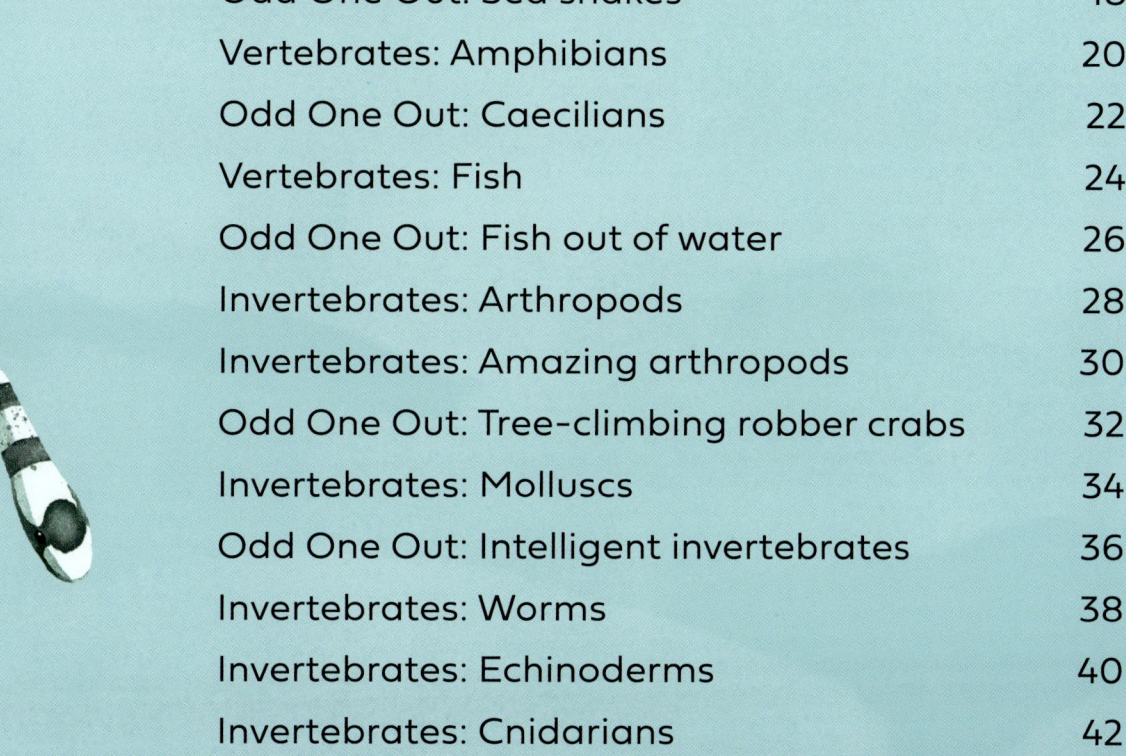

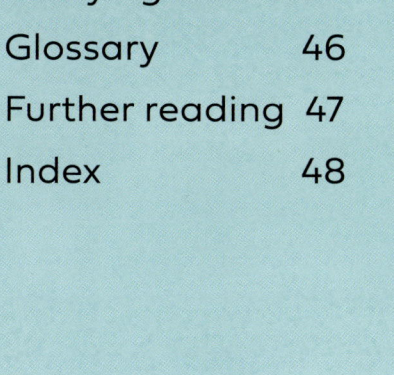

WHAT ARE ANIMALS?

Animals are so familiar. We see them every day – birds flying overhead, cats prowling the streets, insects fluttering in bushes – but do we really know what animals are and how they live? What makes an animal an 'animal'?

Animals can move around

Animals can walk, run, jump, glide, fly and swim. Some, such as coral and mussels, move around when they are young but stay put when they are older.

Flying squirrel

African buffalo

Animals eat other living things

Some animals eat plants and are known as herbivores, and some eat other animals and are called carnivores. The omnivores eat a bit of both.

Great white shark

Most animals breathe in oxygen and give out carbon dioxide

Most land animals have lungs, and most sea and freshwater animals have gills.

Pacific giant octopus

Animals have sensory cells

They can see, hear, taste and touch things, although not all animals have all of these senses. Most also have nerves that connect the senses with the muscles. Many have a brain to control what's going on in different parts of the body.

A world of animals

There are about 1.5 million types of animal described by science, of which a million are insects. There could be another 5.5 million animals waiting to be discovered and classified.

GET YOUR ANIMALS IN ORDER!

Scientists are organised people! They gather together the different types of animal that share similar features and place them in groups. Each group is given a name that describes some of the features shared by the group. The meaning of 'arthropod', for example, is 'jointed foot', referring to how the hard outside skeleton of insects and spiders is clearly divided into segments, including their jointed legs. By classifying them in an ordered fashion, scientists can write and talk about all the known species in the **animal kingdom** without getting them mixed up.

Vertebrates and invertebrates

The animal kingdom can also be divided into two large groups: invertebrates (animals without backbones) and vertebrates (animals with a backbone). Invertebrates include about 30 major groups, such as sponges, molluscs and arthropods. Vertebrates consist of five major groups: mammals, birds, reptiles, amphibians and fish.

Chimpanzees

SPECIES

GENUS

FAMILY

Species

The basic animal grouping is **species**, identified by two names in Latin or Greek – the genus and specific names – and written in italics. An example is *Homo* (genus) *sapiens* (specific), the scientific name for modern people, which means 'wise human'.

Family

Species are grouped together into **families**. Humans join the other great apes – chimpanzees, bonobos, gorillas, and orangutans – in the family Hominidae.

ORDER

CLASS

PHYLUM

KINGDOM

Grey wolf

Bald uakari

Lancelets

Order

Families are grouped into **orders**. The apes, including us, unite with monkeys, lemurs, bush babies and lorises in the order Primates.

Class

Orders are grouped into **classes**. The primates, together with cats, wolves, whales, platypuses and a whole host of animals that have fur and suckle their young are grouped together in the class Mammalia.

Phylum

Classes are grouped into **phyla** (singular: **phylum**). Our human phylum is the Chordata, animals that at some time during their life cycle have a rod of cartilage supporting the back, which eventually develops into a backbone.

Kingdom

Phyla are grouped into **kingdoms**. We are in the animal kingdom. The number of kingdoms has varied down the ages, but scientists today generally recognise that there are six kingdoms – **Animals, Plants, Fungi, Bacteria, Archaea and Protists** – and the animal kingdom is the subject of this book.

MAMMALS

Mammals are furry animals. Even some whales and elephants have a few hairs! Many other mammals have a LOT of hair or fur, which helps keep them warm. Mammals can also control their body temperature, so they are said to be 'warm-blooded'.

African elephant

Mammal milk

Mammals give birth to live young. All female mammals suckle their new-born babies, feeding them milk to help them grow strong, and an elephant mother is no exception. Like a human child, an elephant baby grows slowly and doesn't reach adulthood until it's 18 years old.

Lion family

Furry lions are in the cat family. They live in groups, called prides, while most other cats live and hunt alone. Lions are also in the mammalian Order Carnivora, which includes bears, raccoons and seals. These all have long, fang-like canine teeth for grabbing prey, or for showing off how powerful they are.

Asiatic lion

Koala

Blue whale

Super spine

Mammals are vertebrates because they have a spinal column made of many vertebrae. The blue whale has the longest spinal column in the world – up to 30 metres.

Marsupial mothers

The koala is a marsupial mammal. At birth, a koala is not much bigger than a jelly bean. To keep safe, the 'joey', as it is known, crawls into a pouch below its mother's belly. There, it drinks milk and continues the rest of its development safely hidden away.

ODD ONE OUT

MAMMAL THAT LAYS EGGS

Almost all mammals give birth, except one group – the monotremes. They lay eggs, like reptiles. The hatchlings, though, feed on their mother's milk just like other mammals, and adults have fur. They live in the wild in Australia and New Guinea, where there are two main types – the platypus and the spiny anteater or echidna.

The platypus is the strangest monotreme. When it was first discovered in 1798, naturalists thought it was a hoax, the work of pranksters who cobbled together bits of different animals. You can see why! The platypus has the beak of a duck, a beaver's tail and feet like an otter!

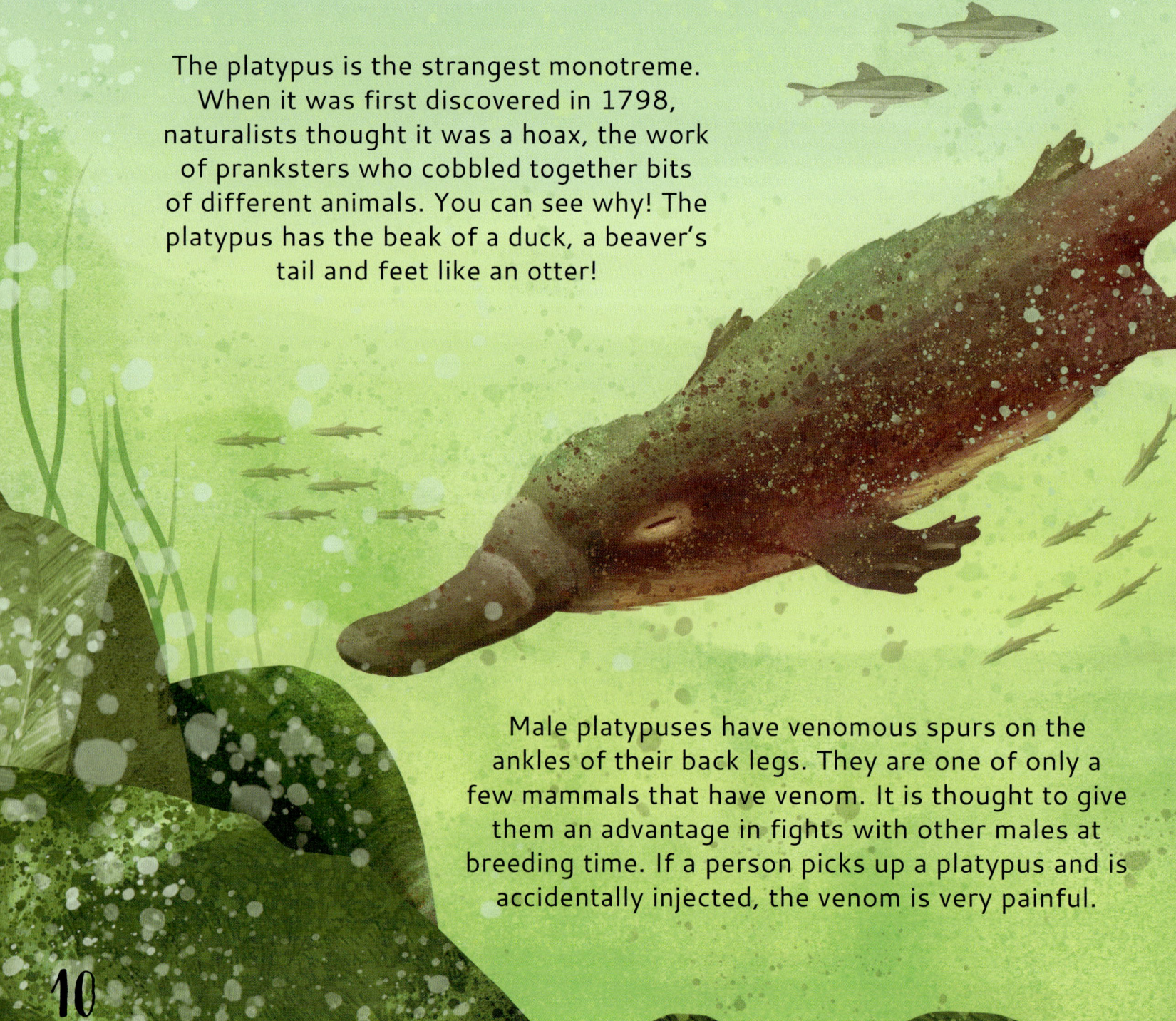

Male platypuses have venomous spurs on the ankles of their back legs. They are one of only a few mammals that have venom. It is thought to give them an advantage in fights with other males at breeding time. If a person picks up a platypus and is accidentally injected, the venom is very painful.

When a platypus dives, it closes it ears, nose and eyes, but it can still find its prey, such as worms and crayfish, at the bottom of streams. It uses a special sense. The front edge of the platypus's beak has receptors that can detect the minute amounts of electricity produced when the muscles of prey contract. It's a way of locating food that they share with sharks and rays, spiny anteaters, and at least one species of dolphin – the Guiana dolphin.

Spiny anteater

In the monotreme group, there are four species of spiny anteater that live in Australia and New Guinea. They have spines like a porcupine and resemble hedgehogs. They are also odd in that their average body temperature is the lowest of any mammal, about 32°C (compared to 37°C in humans), and it rises and falls during the day similar to the temperature of a reptile.

BIRDS

Birds are animals with two legs and claws on their feet. Most have two wings and can fly. Their bodies have a strong but lightweight skeleton and they are covered with feathers. Some feathers keep the bird warm, while others help it fly or are used in displays that scare off rivals and impress potential partners. Birds are warm-blooded so they can control their body temperature without having to warm up in the sun. They also lay eggs with hard shells.

Macaw

Bee-eater

To fly where the sun never sets

Many birds migrate great distances across the world to fly to and from feeding and breeding sites. The longest migration is undertaken by the Arctic tern, which flies between the Arctic and Antarctic each year, a round trip of up to 90,000 km.

Arctic tern

Peregrine falcon

Speedy flyer

Some birds fly fast, others slow. Peregrine falcons can dive, or stoop, at speeds of 320 km/h, the fastest animal on the planet. They do this by folding their wings and using gravity to drop out of the sky.

Land birds

Some birds don't fly. The ostrich has wings, but doesn't use them to fly. It gets about with very powerful legs that propel it along at speeds of 70 km/h. Its wings can act like stabilisers, when it wants to turn at speed, or they can shade ostrich chicks from the sun. Other non-fliers on land include emus, rheas and kiwis.

Ostrich

Bills and beaks

Birds have beaks, also known as bills. Their shape is often linked to what they eat. Finches have short, tough beaks for crushing seeds. Herons have long, pointed beaks to stab at fish, and pelicans have a pouch to scoop them up. Eagles have hooked beaks for tearing meat, and woodpeckers have reinforced beaks for hammering bark to get at the insects underneath.

Hummingbird

Spoonbill

Pelican

Flamingo

Dino-birds

Birds evolved directly from meat-eating dinosaurs, and scientists believe that birds are dinosaurs that survived the mass extinction caused by an asteroid hitting the Earth 66 million years ago. Just think: the sparrows in your garden are actually tiny dinosaurs!

Sparrow

ODD ONE OUT
BIRDS WITH FLIPPERS

Penguins don't have wings. Instead, their front limbs have turned into flippers, so they can swim and dive beneath the waves. They have tightly packed feathers and fat beneath the skin to keep them warm, so many species of penguins can live in cold polar seas.

The largest living penguins are the emperor penguins, at about a metre tall. They live in Antarctica and feed in the stormy Southern Ocean, where they can dive down to 535 metres deep for up to 20 minutes to catch squid and fish.

The smallest penguins are fairy or little penguins that are found on islands off the shores of Australia and New Zealand. They spend most of their life at sea, only coming back for breeding and moulting. They have their chicks in burrows, safe from predatory flying birds.

Rockhopper penguins can be easily recognised because they have red eyes, yellow eyebrows and crests of yellow feathers above their eyes. They get their name from their habit of hopping up steep cliffs with both their feet together.

Giant penguin fossils

About 40 million years ago, there lived a penguin that was as tall as people. Its fossil bones have been found in Antarctica. It's thought it could dive deeper and for longer than emperor penguins, staying down for 40 minutes. It probably became extinct because it had to compete for food with increasing numbers of dolphins and small whales.

REPTILES

Reptiles are scaly animals. Waterproof scales cover their entire bodies. Most are cold-blooded and bask in the sun to warm up, but one or two, such as the leatherback sea turtle, can keep their body temperature a bit higher than their surroundings. Many reptiles lay soft-shelled eggs, which they incubate by burying them in sand or in piles of vegetation, although a few give birth to miniature versions of themselves. There are five main groups: lizards, snakes, turtles and tortoises, crocodiles and alligators and, all on its own, the tuatara.

Crocodile families

Crocodiles, alligators, caiman and gharials live partly on land and partly in water. Crocodiles have long V-shaped snouts, while alligators and caiman have shorter U-shaped snouts, and gharials have long, slender snouts. Their long and powerful tails propel them through water and when they get too hot, they sit with their mouth open to lose heat.

Crocodile

Alligator

Gharial

Leopard gecko

Lizards and dragons

Lizards walk or run on four legs, although the basilisk and frilled lizard sometimes run on their back legs. Most have a long tail. If a predator grabs it, some lizards can discard their tail and regrow it later. They range in size from tiny chameleons a few centimetres long to the 3-metre-long Komodo dragon.

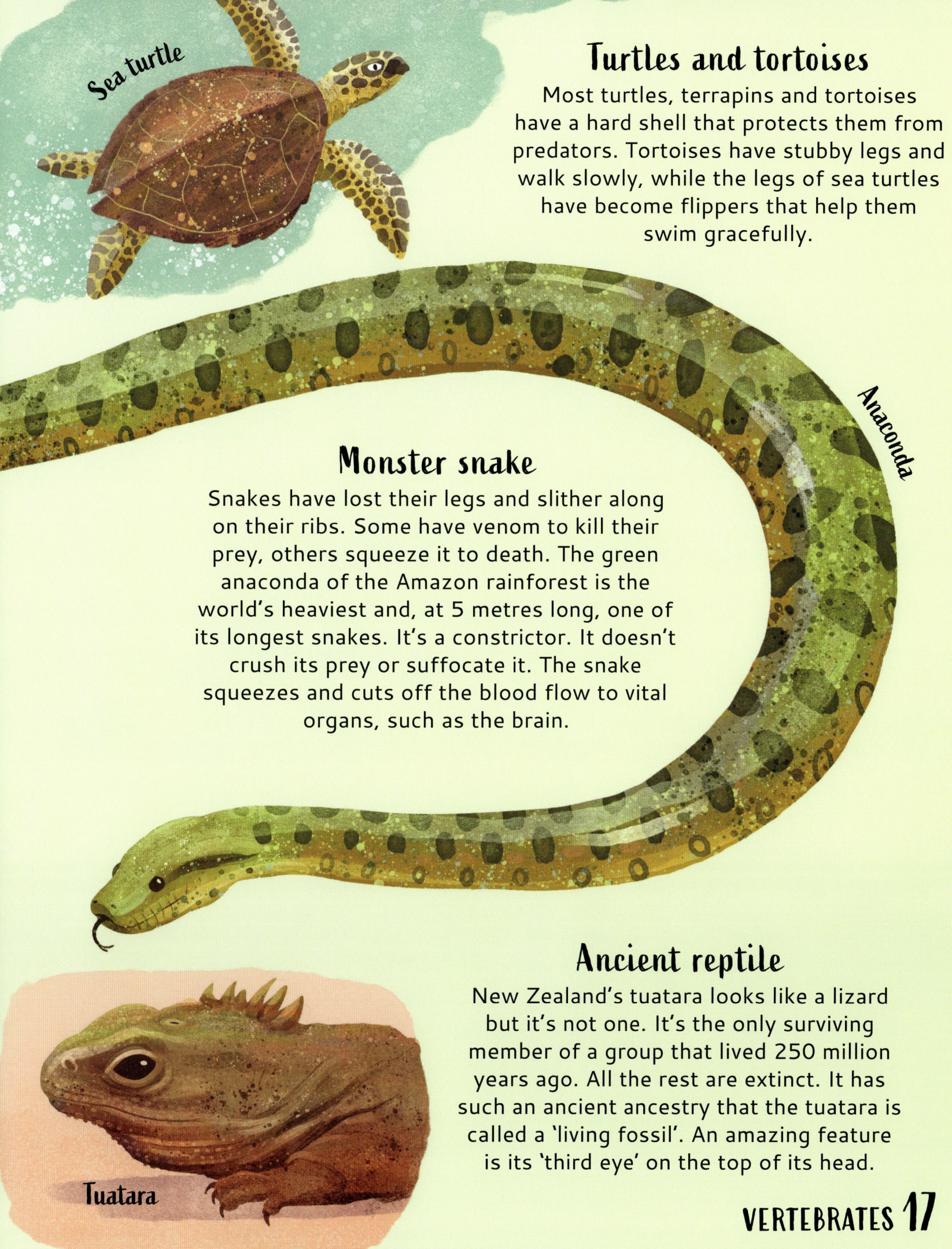

Turtles and tortoises

Most turtles, terrapins and tortoises have a hard shell that protects them from predators. Tortoises have stubby legs and walk slowly, while the legs of sea turtles have become flippers that help them swim gracefully.

Sea turtle

Anaconda

Monster snake

Snakes have lost their legs and slither along on their ribs. Some have venom to kill their prey, others squeeze it to death. The green anaconda of the Amazon rainforest is the world's heaviest and, at 5 metres long, one of its longest snakes. It's a constrictor. It doesn't crush its prey or suffocate it. The snake squeezes and cuts off the blood flow to vital organs, such as the brain.

Ancient reptile

New Zealand's tuatara looks like a lizard but it's not one. It's the only surviving member of a group that lived 250 million years ago. All the rest are extinct. It has such an ancient ancestry that the tuatara is called a 'living fossil'. An amazing feature is its 'third eye' on the top of its head.

Tuatara

ODD ONE OUT

SEA SNAKES

Most reptiles lay their eggs or give birth on land. Sea snakes are the exception. All but one type of sea snake give birth to live young at sea. In fact, most sea snakes are so adapted to a life at sea that they are unable to move on land.

Some sea snakes have special sensory organs on their heads that detect the movements of fish, which they try to catch.

Sea snakes breathe air like all reptiles but have their nostrils towards the top of the head. These have valves to exclude water. They can also breathe through their skin.

Sea snakes have paddle-like tails for efficient swimming.

Sea snakes are active both day and night. They are sometimes seen basking in the sun at the surface, and they have been seen at depths of 100 metres, where they can hunt for several hours on a single breath.

Snake survival

Most sea snake mothers have eggs in their body from which baby snakes hatch. After a few months, the mother expels the live snakes from her body into the sea. From then on, the baby snakes must survive on their own. They are born fully developed so they can see, hear, move and hunt straight away.

Sea snakes are among the most venomous snakes in the world, but they rarely bite people.

19

AMPHIBIANS

Amphibians were the first tetrapods – animals with four legs. They evolved over 400 million years ago from fish. The fish's fins became legs, and the young of many amphibians still have gills just like fish. Nowadays, most amphibians live part of their life in water and the rest on land. The adults have lungs with which to breathe air, although when in water, they can also take in oxygen through their skin. There are three main groups: frogs and toads, salamanders and newts, and caecilians.

Close to water

Most amphibians have skin without scales, and they must keep it damp. Some toads do not. They have a dry and warty skin and have poison glands that exude nasty chemicals to protect themselves from predators.

Common toad

Surinam toad

Amphibian babies

Almost all amphibians lay their eggs in water. Some frogs and toads lay their eggs in large masses, known as spawn. The eggs develop into tadpoles. Others lay them one at a time and carry the tadpoles to water on their backs or make a nest of foam to protect them. The Surinam toad mother even has little pouches on her back in which the eggs and tadpoles develop.

Freezing frogs

Amphibians are cold-blooded so they have adaptations that enable them to survive in the cold. In North America, the wood frog's habitat is a frozen wilderness in winter, and so it shuts down its body and hibernates, just like many other amphibians. But it also has another trick. When its pond freezes, it freezes too, not totally solid, but almost solid, and then it thaws out in spring.

Wood frog

Alpine newt

Newts and salamanders

Newts spend almost all their time in water and have tails like fish. Many salamanders live most of their lives on land and look a bit like lizards. Some have skin glands that produce deadly poisons.

Fossil amphibian monster

Before there were dinosaurs, there were giant amphibians. *Prionosuchus* would dwarf all of today's amphibians were it still alive. It lived about 285 million years ago, looked more like a crocodile than an amphibian and was 9 metres long. Today, the largest living amphibian is the 1.8-metre-long Chinese giant salamander.

Chinese giant salamander

ODD ONE OUT
CAECILIANS

The strangest amphibian must be the caecilian. It has no legs, so small ones look like earthworms, and large ones resemble snakes. Most caecilians live underground. The head has plates of bone joined in such a way to act like a shovel so they can burrow through the soil. Others live in water.

Living underground, most caecilians have no need to see, so they have small eyes or eyes hidden under the skin.

Caecilians detect predators and prey by picking up vibrations in the ground. They have tiny sensitive tentacles between the nostrils and the eyes to find food and their way around.

Caecilians have sharp teeth. They mostly eat insects and worms. They will also catch other amphibians and even eat other caecilians.

Scraping the outside

One type of caecilian mother lives in Kenya and lays eggs, and she feeds her hatchlings in a very unusual way. They eat a special layer of skin, containing fats and proteins, which the mother grows on the outside of her body. The youngsters peel it off with modified teeth.

Some caecilian mothers lay eggs in damp holes near water, while others give birth to live young.

The longest caecilian is 2.4 metres long, and the shortest is 9 centimetres.

FISH

There are three main types of fish: sharks and rays with skeletons made out of bendy cartilage; bony fish with a rigid skeleton of bone; and hagfish and lampreys that have no jaws. Most have scales and, those that don't, have a layer of slime all over their body instead.

Fish and fins

Fish move and stay upright with the aid of fins. Many fish use the tail fin for movement, while the dorsal fin keeps them from tilting to one side. The pectoral fins are shaped like wings, especially those on sharks. They help the fish to glide though the water.

Lionfish

Butterfly fish

Clown fish

Blue tang

Up and down

Many fish can adjust their buoyancy. Bony fish have an air-filled swim bladder. Add more air and they float upwards. Take some away and they sink. Sharks have a large, oily liver. Oil is lighter than water, so it helps to keep the shark buoyant.

Breathing underwater

Fish breathe with gills. Oxygen in the water passes across the surface of the gill and into the blood. It is then carried around the body in the bloodstream.

Stingray

Sixth sense

Fish have good senses of smell, taste and touch. They all have a line of sensors along each side of the body, known as the lateral line, which picks up vibrations in the water — a kind of 'touch at a distance'. Sharks and rays have a special sixth sense. Sensors in their snout can detect the tiny amounts of electricity in the muscles of their prey.

Ocean giants

The largest fish in the sea — whale sharks, basking sharks, and manta rays — feed on some of the smallest. They are all filter feeders. They sift plankton and small fish from the water. Whale sharks are huge, up to 9 metres long, and the oceanic manta ray has 'wings' 7 metres across.

Basking shark

Jawless fish

Hagfish and lampreys are shaped like eels, have no scales and no jaws. Their mouth is round and filled with small teeth. Lampreys attach with their mouth to larger fish and suck their blood. Hagfish feed on dead bodies. When hagfish are attacked they produce huge amounts of slime that gums up the gills of their attacker.

Lamprey

ODD ONE OUT

FISH OUT OF WATER

Mudskippers are fish that behave like amphibians. They're built to move on land. The pectoral fins are further forward and under the body than in other fish, so they can function like legs. By flicking its tail, the fish is able to 'skip' across the beach and even climb low-growing trees! Its eyes protrude from the top of its head so it can see across the beach.

Mudskippers must keep damp in order to breathe. They absorb oxygen through the skin, and through the lining of the mouth and throat. They can trap a bubble of moist air in their gills, so the gills can also help them breathe while out of the water.

Mudskippers live in burrows, which they closely guard from other mudskippers. When the tide is high, they hide in their burrows, but when it goes out, they appear on the surface of the mud or sand.

Walkers and flyers

Several other fish come out of the water. The climbing perch can be out for up to 10 hours and walk from one pond or ditch to another. It 'walks' with its tail and uses spines on the edge of its gill covers to dig into the ground and hold it steady. Moray eels shoot out of rock pools to grab crabs, and flying fish shoot out of the ocean and glide over the sea's surface to escape predators chasing them from below.

The male mudskipper attracts females with boisterous displays, such as raising the dorsal fin like a flag, and lifting its body up on its tail and flopping back down — anything to impress a potential partner. If he's successful, the female will deposit her eggs in his burrow, and he will guard them until they hatch.

27

ARTHROPODS

Arthropods are invertebrate animals with jointed legs, segmented bodies and an exoskeleton (outside skeleton). There are four main groups: insects, arachnids (spiders, mites and scorpions), centipedes and millipedes and crustaceans.

A lot of them

Arthropods make up about 84 per cent of all the animals on Earth, and they live in every type of habitat on the planet. They walk, run and swim and, about 400 million years ago, insects were the first animals to fly.

Lobster

Lots of legs

While many animals have four limbs, arthropods have more. Insects have six legs, spiders and scorpions have eight, centipedes have 15 to 177, but always an odd number of pairs, and the leggiest millipede, from California, USA, has up to 750 legs! Crabs and lobsters have ten legs, the first two modified as claws. Shrimps and prawns have ten walking legs and ten 'swimming legs'.

Shrimps

Armoured sea creatures

The ocean is the domain of crustaceans, although a few live in freshwater and on land. While most arthropods are small, crustaceans in the sea can grow very big, like the Japanese spider crab that has a leg span of 3.7 metres. The smallest crustaceans, such as krill and copepods, are important sources of food for many marine animals.

Japanese spider crab

Parasites

Three of the four main arthropod groups have parasites in their ranks. Fleas and lice are wingless insects. Ticks and mites are arachnids. Whale lice and the tongue-eating louse are crustaceans. There are no parasitic centipedes or millipedes.

Fleas

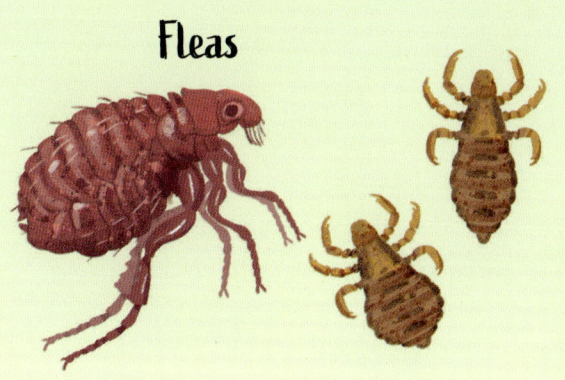

AMAZING ARTHROPODS

With their armour-like exoskeleton, arthropods must grow in an unusual way. First they split their hard 'skin' and walk out of it. Then, while their skin is soft, they grow a bit. Finally, the new skin hardens and they are little bit bigger than they were before.

Transformations

Insects change in shape and behaviour from one stage of their life cycle to the next, a process known as metamorphosis. Locusts and dragonflies have incomplete metamorphosis – egg, nymph and adult. Bees and butterflies have complete metamorphosis – egg, larva (caterpillar), pupa (chrysalis) and adult. The nymph and caterpillar stages are mainly when they feed and grow.

Monarch butterflies

Darwin's bark spider

Mega-webs

Spiders produce one of the toughest materials in nature – silk. Size for size, spider silk is tougher than fine steel. Many spiders spin a web of silk to trap prey, and the web of Darwin's bark spider is by far the biggest and toughest. Its anchor lines can span 25 metres across rivers, and the web itself covers three square metres.

Environmental aids

Arthropods keep the environment healthy. Bees, beetles, moths and flies pollinate plants. Burying beetles deal with dead bodies. Dung beetles have a use for dung (they lay their eggs in it so the youngsters have something to eat when they hatch out). Silk moths provide us with silk for clothes. Insects are also generally food for many other animals.

Silk moth

Venoms and poisons

Many arthropods have either venom or poison for protection. Venom is injected, poison is eaten. Bees, wasps and ants have venomous stingers, as do scorpions.

Centipedes inject venom with their formidable jaw-like front legs.

Bombardier beetles squirt boiling hot liquids from their rear end.

Stinkbugs release an unpleasant smelling spray if touched.

ODD ONE OUT

TREE-CLIMBING ROBBER CRABS

Not all crabs live in the sea. Some thrive in rivers and streams, while others spend most of their life on land. Many land-based crabs must always visit the sea at some point in their life cycle, as their eggs and larvae need to be in the ocean to develop.

Giant land crab

At up to a metre across from one leg tip to another, the robber or coconut crab is the world's largest land-based arthropod. Robber crabs have a good sense of smell. They use it to find ripe fruits, nuts and carrion (dead bodies); in fact, they will eat just about anything, including somebody's lunch, which led to them being called 'robber crabs'.

Coconut crab

Robber crabs sometimes climb palm trees and accidentally dislodge ripe coconuts, hence their alternative name 'coconut crab'. They climb trees mainly to escape from predatory birds and larger robber crabs that might eat them.

A life on land

If robber crabs are washed out to sea, they cannot swim and will drown. Female crabs, though, have to go to the edge of the sea to release their eggs. The eggs hatch in the sea, and the larvae float about in the plankton.

All at sea

After three to four weeks, they settle on the seabed and place their soft abdomens in sea snail shells. When they have grown enough, the young robber crabs clamber onto the land and, as they get older, the abdomen develops a tough exoskeleton, and they abandon their shell. They must must remain on land for the rest of their life.

33

MOLLUSCS

Molluscs come in all sorts of different shapes and sizes, but the one thing that unites them is a mantle. The muscular mantle is the outer wall of a mollusc's body. It encloses all the inner organs. It can also form tubes that can be used for feeding or movement.

Molluscs and shells

Many molluscs have shells. Snails are gastropod molluscs, which means they move with the help of a single large foot and carry a shell on their back. Many gastropods have a single spiral shell, while bivalves have a pair of hinged shells. Shells help to protect the animal from predators. Even squid have a shell, but it's on the inside and called a quill. It functions like a backbone, supporting the squid's body.

Giant squid

Two shells

The mussel is a bivalve mollusc. It has two shells held tightly together by strong muscles. To anchor itself to the seabed it secretes strong anchor ropes called byssal threads or beard. The mussel feeds by sucking in water through a tube, called a siphon, and filtering out plankton, before squirting out the water through another siphon.

Mussels

Colourful naked molluscs

Nudibranchs are gastropod molluscs without shells, and they all live in the sea. They usually have a rosette of 'naked gills' on their back, and some species have rows of horn–shaped outgrowths, known as cerata. Some nudibranchs eat and then store the stinging cells of jellyfish or Portuguese man o' war in a small sac at the tip of their cerata, and they can use them as a defence against predators.

Coat-of-mail shells

Chitons or coat–of–mail shells are marine molluscs with a flat shell on their back, composed of eight overlapping shell plates. Some chitons have a remarkable homing ability. They wander off across the rocks but always return to the exact same spot.

Nudibranchs

Chitons

ODD ONE OUT

INTELLIGENT INVERTEBRATES

The class of cephalopods includes octopuses, squid and cuttlefish. They have a prominent head with a big brain. An octopus has eight arms. Squid and cuttlefish have eight arms and two tentacles. They all have a siphon that is used for jet propulsion or to squirt ink as a smokescreen. Many can change the colour, pattern and texture of their skin in an instant, either to match their background or to communicate.

Tool users

Compared to other molluscs, cephalopod molluscs are highly intelligent animals. In an aquarium, octopuses can learn to pick out shapes and patterns, and in the wild they use tools. The veined octopus takes coconut shells to construct a protective 'house', and common octopuses gather shells and stones about them. It's a kind of armour to defend themselves against sharks.

Skin talk

Squid talk to each other using their skin and have their own language. It's a visual language of changing patterns of stripes and dots, but scientists have yet to work out the detail of what they are saying. Some conversations are related to courtship, but most are a mystery. The large and ferocious Humboldt squid even has light-producing organs in its muscles. They provide a backlight, like an e-book reader, so a squid can talk to other squid even in the dark.

Animal magicians

The cuttlefish uses rapidly shifting skin patterns to hypnotise its prey. It then shoots out its pair of long tentacles and grabs the prey before it has a chance to escape. The cuttlefish can also send out two different messages at the same time. On one side of its body, it can warn off a rival, while on the other side, it can be trying to impress a potential mate.

WORMS

Many worms are long, hollow tubes or ribbons. There are many different kinds: segmented worms, flatworms, round worms, ribbon worms, spoon worms and bristle worms. They vary in size from one-millimetre-long roundworms to 30-metre-long ribbon worms, perhaps the longest animals on Earth.

Earthworm

Earthworm

The earthworm is a segmented worm. It burrows into the soil and is important in keeping the soil fertile. There are many types, but Australia's giant Gippsland earthworms are the longest, at up to 3 metres long.

Feather dusters

One of the most beautiful worms must be the fan worm. It looks like a colourful feather duster. A fan worm lives in a tube from which its crown of feathery feeding tentacles protrudes. These filter the seawater for food particles.

Fan worms

A class of parasites

The tapeworm is a ribbon-like flatworm parasite. It lives inside another animal, called the host, and does it harm. The tapeworm lives in the intestine, where it absorbs food, so the host goes hungry. It has a head and neck, called a scolex, which has tiny hooks to attach it to the gut wall of its host. The neck continually produces detachable body units containing eggs that are transported outside in the host's droppings, and eventually find their way into a new host.

Tapeworm

Sand striker

The bobbit worm is a fearsome predator. It is a bristle worm that buries its three-metre-long iridescent body in the sand. Just its head and formidable jaws stick out. If a fish or shrimp passes, the worm grabs it, pulls it down below the sand and eats it.

Bobbit worm

ECHINODERMS

Many echinoderms have a covering of spines, and most have a five-star body shape. There are sea urchins, starfish, brittle stars, feather stars, sea lilies, basket stars and sea cucumbers.

Spiny stars

Starfish or sea stars generally have five arms, but they can have more. Antarctica's 'deathstar' has up to 50 slender arms. Starfish move with hundreds of tiny tube feet on the underside of their body. When they feed, their stomach comes out of their body and engulfs the prey.

Deathstar starfish

Inside a sea urchin

Spiny balls

Sea urchins are globular, but you can still see the five-star arrangement etched into the test or 'shell'. The mouth on its underside has five pyramid-shaped teeth that can be used to scrape, tear and grind food, such as kelp or sponges.

Spiny flowers

Many sea lilies or crinoids are attached to the seabed, although some species can move about. They have a crown of feathery arms covered in tube feet with which they trap food.

Sea lilies

Deep-sea sausages

Sea cucumbers are mainly sausage-shaped soft-bodied echinoderms, but there are some unusual ones in the deep sea. Little 'sea pigs' live on the seabed and the 'headless chickens' swim above them.

Headless chicken sea cucumber

Sea cucumber

Sea pig

CNIDARIANS

The body of a cnidarian or 'sea jelly' consists of a jelly-like substance sandwiched between two layers of cells. Many have tentacles covered in stinging cells, which are used to capture prey.

Reef builders

Reef-building coral polyps secrete calcium carbonate (limestone) to form coral reefs. Inside their tissues live tiny creatures, known as zooxanthellae, which give the coral its colour. They harness the energy from the Sun to make food (photosynthesis) and share it with the coral.

Flowers in the sea

Sea anemones consist of a small column of tissue topped with a ring of tentacles. Most remain attached to rocks and rarely move, although most can move if they have to. The onion anemone can roll into a ball and lets the ocean currents move it about until it finds a muddy seabed to settle on.

Sea anemone

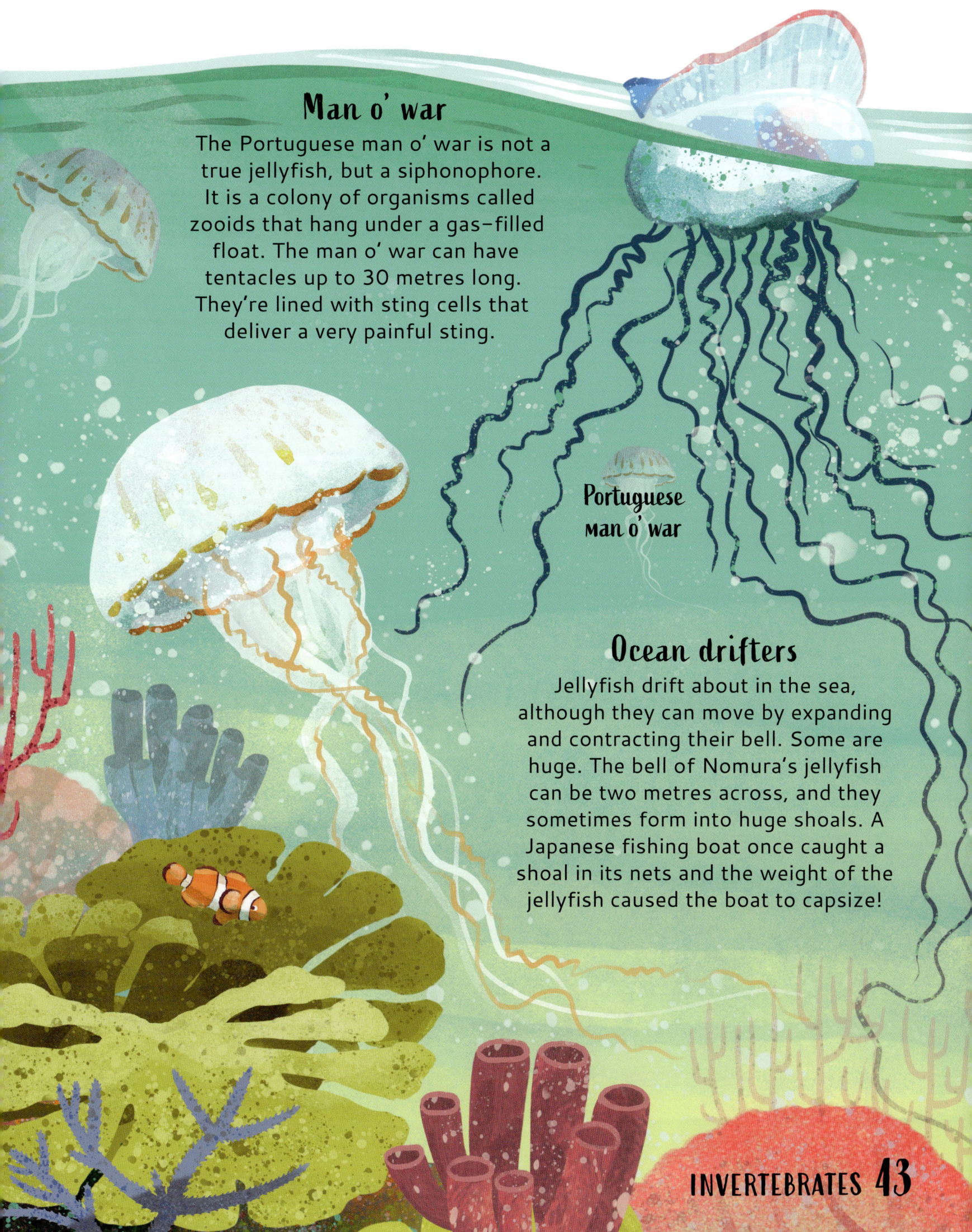

Man o' war

The Portuguese man o' war is not a true jellyfish, but a siphonophore. It is a colony of organisms called zooids that hang under a gas-filled float. The man o' war can have tentacles up to 30 metres long. They're lined with sting cells that deliver a very painful sting.

Portuguese man o' war

Ocean drifters

Jellyfish drift about in the sea, although they can move by expanding and contracting their bell. Some are huge. The bell of Nomura's jellyfish can be two metres across, and they sometimes form into huge shoals. A Japanese fishing boat once caught a shoal in its nets and the weight of the jellyfish caused the boat to capsize!

STUDYING ANIMALS

The study of animals is a branch of biology called zoology, and scientists who study the animal kingdom are known as zoologists.

A zoology timeline

· **17,000 years ago.** Animals have fascinated people since the dawn of modern humans. The earliest cave paintings, like those at Lascaux in southwest France, are of animals with which the artists were familiar – wild cattle, bison, deer, horses, bears, cats and birds.

· **The ancient Greek philosopher Aristotle** (384–322 BCE) was one of the first zoologists. He recognised about 500 different species of animal and wrote about them in his *History of Animals*. People have called him the 'father of zoology'.

· **In 1758**, the Swedish biologist Carl Linnaeus published the tenth edition of his *Systema Naturae*, which was the origin of the two-name system of classifying animals that we use today.

· **In 1858**, groundbreaking ideas from Charles Darwin and Alfred Russel Wallace were presented to the Linnean Society in London. They gave rise to the theory of evolution that Darwin later wrote about in *On the Origin of Species*.

· **In 1960**, zoologist Jane Goodall studied chimpanzees at Gombe, East Africa and discovered that they not only use tools to 'fish' for termites, but also engaged in armed warfare.

· **In 1962**, Rachel Carson published her book *Silent Spring* drawing attention to the way birds were being poisoned by man-made chemicals. It was the dawn of the environmental movement and the realisation that people are not taking care of the planet.

· **In 1973**, Konrad Lorenz, Nikolaas Tinbergen and Karl von Frisch shared the Nobel Prize for their pioneering studies on the behaviour of animals. Lorenz studied instinctive behaviour in geese by getting them to follow him about Tinbergen recorded the behaviour of gulls, and von Frisch interpreted the dance language of honeybees.

· **In 2020**, Jennifer Doudna and Emmanuel Charpentier were awarded the Nobel Prize for their work on editing or reprogramming genes, what some scientists consider to be the most important advance ever in the field of biology. In agriculture and food production it will change the plants and animals that we eat, and in medicine it will help prevent diseases. It is something that is likely to change the world.

Why study animals?

It is important to study animals for all sorts of reasons, not least because we want to understand how the world and its wildlife are getting on. One subject that is important in current animal research is biodiversity. Biodiversity is about the variety of life that you find in a particular place – all the animals, plants, fungi and bacteria. It is useful to know, for instance, just how many animals are living there. When their populations increase or decrease, it gives scientists a clear indication of the health of that habitat.

Nothing, though, lives alone. All the plants, animals and microbes depend on each other. Each is part of a complex ecosystem. If one living thing is absent from the system, many others are affected too. The problem today is that animal populations are falling all over the world, and some of the places they live are slowly disappearing.

A report published by the Worldwide Fund for Nature (WWF) highlighted that there has been a 60 per cent decline in the global populations of vertebrates – mammals, birds, reptiles, amphibians and fish – since 1970. This is due partly to loss of habitat, such as the cutting down of forests to be replaced by food crops, and partly due to other factors, such as the way that the planet is warming up due to human activities.

Some animals can adapt to change. These are the generalists, like rats and cockroaches, which have adapted to live alongside humans. The specialists, such as polar bears, which depend on there being sea ice in the Arctic to be able to hunt, are less able to adapt, and so are threatened with extinction. Another WWF report revealed that over a million animal and plant species are threatened with extinction, the highest number in human history.

With about 5.5 million species of animals still to be discovered, we could be losing species before we even knew they existed at all. However, by studying animals and their surroundings, there is the possibility we can start to put things right.

GLOSSARY

abdomen one section of an animal's body

aquatic living in water

buoyancy the ability to float or move up and down in water

canine like a dog or related to dogs

carnivore an animal that eats other animals

cartilage bendy material like that in your nose and outer ear

cell the basic unit of a living thing that can copy itself independently of any other living thing

classification the arrangement of plants and animals into formal groups based on their similarities

dorsal fin a fin located on the top of fish

extinct when a type of animal dies out and has gone forever

gills the organs used for breathing by fish and other animals that live in water

glands a group of cells or an organ that produces fluids that are released into the body

globular globe-shaped

gravity the force by which all objects are attracted to each other

herbivore an animal that eats plants

incubate to keep warm until eggs hatch

invertebrate animal without a backbone

iridescent shiny and brightly coloured

larva young stage in an animal's life between egg and adult

omnivore animal that eats both plants and animals

organism an individual plant, animal, fungus, protist or bacterium

mass extinction when many plants and animals became extinct at the same time

parasite plant or animal that lives on or inside another plant or animal

pectoral fins a pair of fins behind a fish's head, helping to control the direction of movement

poison a substance that can kill or seriously harm living things

photosynthesis the process by which green plants and other organisms manufacture sugars from carbon dioxide and water using the energy from the Sun.

plankton living things that drift in oceans or lakes

polyp the living part of coral, which resembles a tiny sea anemone

predator an animal that hunts and eats other animals

prey an animal that is hunted and eaten by another animal

species a group of similar individuals of plants or animals that can breed together. Their scientific name is written as two Latin words in italics, e.g. *Homo sapiens*

tentacles long, thin parts of an animal for holding or feeling things

tissues a collection of specialised cells in the body of a plant or animal, such as muscle or nerves

tropical living in a hot region of the Earth, located in a broad band either side of the Equator

venom a poisonous substance produced by animals that is injected into prey or an attacker by biting or stinging

vertebrate animal with a backbone

warty growths on the surface of skin

womb the place in a mother mammal's body where the unborn baby develops

FURTHER READING

Above, Below and Long Ago by Michael Bright (Wayland, 2022)

Animal Tongues; Animal Tails by Tim Cooke (Wayland, 2022)

A World Full of Wildlife by Neal Layton (Wren and Rook, 2023)

Darwin's Tree of Life by Michael Bright (Wayland, 2019)

The Variety of Life by Nicola Davies (Hodder Children's Books, 2017)

INDEX